非暴力沟通・养育篇

[美]马歇尔・卢森堡 Marshall B. Rosenberg ◎著
刘畅◎译 李迪◎审校

Raising Children Compassionately

图书在版编目（CIP）数据

非暴力沟通.养育篇/（美）马歇尔·卢森堡（Marshall B.Rosenberg）著；刘畅译.—北京：华夏出版社有限公司，2021.7（2023.11重印）

（非暴力沟通系列）

书名原文：Raising Children Compassionately: Parenting the Nonviolent Communication Way

ISBN 978-7-5222-0070-5

Ⅰ.①非… Ⅱ.①马…②刘… Ⅲ.①家庭教育 Ⅳ.① G4

中国版本图书馆 CIP 数据核字（2020）第 268338 号

Translated from the book Raising Children Compassionately by Marshall Rosenberg

Copyright © 2004 PuddleDancer Press, published by PuddleDancer Press. All rights reserved. Used with permission. For further information about Nonviolent Communication(TM) please visit the Center for Nonviolent Communication on the Web at: www.cnvc.org

版权所有，翻印必究。
北京市版权局著作权合同登记号：图字 01-2018-2560 号

非暴力沟通·养育篇

作　　者	［美］马歇尔·卢森堡
译　　者	刘　畅
责任编辑	王凤梅
责任印制	刘　洋
出版发行	华夏出版社有限公司
经　　销	新华书店
印　　刷	三河市少明印务有限公司
装　　订	三河市少明印务有限公司
版　　次	2021 年 7 月北京第 1 版　2023 年 11 月北京第 2 次印刷
开　　本	787×1092　1/32 开
印　　张	4.25
字　　数	30 千字
定　　价	49.00 元

华夏出版社有限公司 　地址：北京市东直门外香河园北里 4 号　邮编：100028
网址：www.hxph.com.cn　电话：(010) 64663331（转）
若发现本版图书有印装质量问题，请与我社营销中心联系调换。

目 录
CONTENTS

引言 … 001

Introduction … 079

我自身的觉察 … 001

My Own Awareness … 080

以家长身份接受的教育 … 005

Our Education As Parents … 082

强制和惩罚的局限 … 009

The Limitations of Coercion and Punishment … 084

有一定品质的连接 … 015

A Certain Quality of Connection … 088

奖励的局限 … 021

The Limitations of Rewards … 091

转变惯性的沟通方式 … 025

Transforming Your Habitual Communication … 093

"家务战争" … 031

"Chore Wars" … 096

无条件的爱 … 037

Unconditional Love … 100

让我们的孩子做好准备 … 043

Preparing Our Children … 103

"船长"游戏 … 049

The "Captain" Game … 106

强制手段的使用 ⋯ 055

The Use of Force ⋯ 109

互助社群 ⋯ 063

Supportive Communities ⋯ 114

非暴力沟通的四个步骤 ⋯ 071

The Four-Part Nonviolent Communication Process ⋯ 120

人类共有的一些基本感受 ⋯ 073

Some Basic Feelings We All Have ⋯ 123

人类共有的一些基本需要 ⋯ 074

Some Basic Needs We All Have ⋯ 124

引 言
以爱养育

向家长们教授非暴力沟通 30 年了,我想分享一些对我和来听课的家长们都很有帮助的东西,以及对养育这一美好又富有挑战的工作的些许见解。

首先,我想提醒大家注意,如果一个人不被称为"孩子",会导致我们对他尊重的程度发生改变,那"孩子"这个词就是危险的。我来解释一下我的意思。

多年来,在我带领的养育工作坊中,课程开始前,我通常会安排这样一个小实验:把参与者分为两组,让他们分别待在不同的房间里,任务是在一张大纸上写下发生冲突时,他们与冲突方的对话。我会告诉所有人这是个怎样的冲突,唯一的不同是,我告诉其中一组,发生冲突的对方是他们的孩子,而告诉另外一组,发生冲突的对方是他们的邻居。

任务完成后我们回到大组,一起看看每个小组记录下的对话概要,一种情况认为对方是他们的孩子,另一种则认为是邻居(我不会让两组人交流他们所面对的冲突方是谁,所以两个小组都以为他们所面对的情境是相同的)。

大家彼此浏览了各自写下的对话后,我问,就对话所呈现的尊重和同情心程度,能否看出有差异。每当这时,大家都会发现,相比冲突方是邻居的那组,孩子这组在沟通中获得的尊重和同情心都要少一些。这一结果令人痛苦,它向在场的家长们表明,仅仅因为对方是"我们的孩子"这个想法,我们就轻易忽略了人性的一面。

我自身的觉察

曾经的一次经历让我更敏锐地意识到，把他人当作孩子对待所带来的危害。那是一个周末，我与街头帮派和警察局这两个组织一同工作，他们之间存在着相当严重的暴力冲突，我的任务就是调解双方冲突。我竭尽所能地花了很长时间调解他们之间的暴力冲突，这之后我精疲力竭。开车回家的路上，我告诉自己：这辈子再也不想处于什么冲突之中了。

然而，到家后，我从后门进屋，发现我的三个孩子正在打架。我以我们在非暴力沟通中所倡导的方式向他们表达我的痛苦。我表达了自己的感受、需要和请求。具体我是这么做的，我大吼道："眼前正在发生的一切，让我感到特别紧张！经历了这么一个周末之后，我真的需要一些平静和安宁！你们大家愿意给我这样的时间和空间吗？"

我最大的儿子看着我说："你想聊聊吗？"那一瞬间，我头脑里忽略了他身上鲜活的人性。为什么这么说呢？因为我告诉自己："看！多可爱，这有个9岁的男孩儿正试图帮助他父亲呢。"没错，我差点儿因为他的年龄而拒绝他的提议。仔细分析，更深层的原因是我给他贴上了"孩子"的标签。幸运的是，我意识到了自己头脑里正在冒出的这个想法，对此我能够觉察得如此清晰，或许是因为在街头帮派和警察局之间进行的调解工作，已经向我展示了从标签而不是人性角度看待他人所带来的危害。

一旦我不再将他当作一个孩子并在心里给他打上"多可爱"的标签，我看到的是，一个人正在对另一个身处痛苦中的人伸出援手。因此，我大声回答："是的，我很想要聊一聊。"于是，三个孩子随我走进另一个房间，倾听我坦陈自己的痛苦。这痛苦来自人们彼此走到互相伤害的地步，仅仅因为他们从未被教授去看到他人身上的人类共性。45分钟后，我感觉好极了，印象中我们还打开了立体声音响，像傻瓜一样跳了一阵子舞。

以家长身份
接受的教育

我并非建议在谈到该年龄段的人时，不要使用诸如"孩子"这样的称谓。我想探讨的是，在我们的文化中，"孩子"这个称谓，会使我们忽略孩子身上的人类共性。在这种情况下，我们往往默许自己被这类标签遮蔽而无法正确看待对方。让我就这部分多说说，"孩子"这个标签会怎样导致我们不幸的行为表现。

关于养育，我受到的教育使我认为，家长的工作就是要让孩子规矩听话。你看，在这种文化里，一旦把自己定义为一个权威，即老师或家长，那么，对那些被贴上"孩子"或"学生"标签的人，管教他们的行为举止，就被视为自己的责任了。

现在我明白，这样的目的会带来怎样事与愿违的结果了。因为我认识到，任何时候，只要目的是要他人以某种特定方式行事，那么，无论我们的请求是什么，人们都倾向于反抗。2岁也好，92岁也好，似乎都是这样。

从他人那里得到我们想要的，或是让他人按照我们的意思去做，这样的目的威胁了他人的自主权——选择自己想要做什么的权利。只要感到对要做的事没有选择的自由，人们都倾向于反抗，即便他们能体会到我们提出请求的用意，即便他们自己通常也会想要这样做。我们保护自主权的需要是如此强烈，以至于如果发现某人特别执着，总是表现得好像只有他们才知道对我们来说什么是最好的，总是不让我们自己决定如何行事，那就会加剧我们的反抗。

强制和惩罚的
局限

我要永远感谢我的孩子们。关于让他人做你想要他做的事，这样的目的带来的局限性，是我的孩子们教育了我。他们教给我的第一件事是，我不能强制他们照我的意思做。我不能强制他们做任何事。我不能强制他们把玩具放回玩具盒子，我不能强制他们整理床铺，我不能强制他们吃东西。作为家长，认识到自己的无能为力，这真是自尊心受挫的一课，毕竟之前我已经形成了这样的思维定式，即教导孩子规矩听话是家长的工作。这就是这些小孩子们给我上的伤自尊的一课，我不能强制他们做任何事。我所能做的仅仅是，让他们后悔之前没按我的意思去做。

每当我傻到这样做时，也就是"让他们后悔之前没按我的意思去做"时，他们就会给我上第二课：关于养育和权力。对我来说，多年来的经历证明了这一课极有价值。这一课就是，任何时候，如果我决定让他们后悔没按我的意思去做，他们就会让我后悔做出这个决定。暴力招致暴力。

他们教给我，任何来自我的强制手段，都一定会招致他们的反抗，这会造成我们双方关系的敌对。我不希望与任何人有这样的敌对关系，尤其不愿意对方是自己的孩子，他们与我如此亲密，而我对他们负有莫大的责任。所以，我最不想与我的孩子陷入这种强制的把戏，而惩罚，就是强制的一部分。

现如今，大部分家长都强烈支持惩罚的观念。研究表明，美国大约有 80% 的家长坚定拥护对孩子进行体罚，这与认为要对罪犯保留死刑的人口比例基本相同。在教育孩子的过程中惩罚是必要且公正的，持此种信念的人占如此高的比例，这使得多年来我有充足的机会可以和家长们就这一问题进行探讨。令我高兴的是，只要问自己两个问题，就能帮助人们认识到，任何形式的惩罚都有局限性。

第一个问题是：我们想要孩子的行为做出怎样的改变？如果我们只问这个问题，那看起来有的时候惩罚的确是有效的，因为通过威胁或者真正实施惩罚，我们确实可以时不时地让孩子按我们的意思去做。

但是，当我们加上第二个问题，以我的经验来看，家长们就会发现惩罚永远都不会起作用。第二个问题就是：我们想要孩子出于什么样的原因按我们希望的方式行事？就是这个问题能帮助我们认识到，惩罚不仅不会起作用，相反，还会阻碍孩子按我们所希望的动机行事。

既然惩罚很常用，并且被认为是正当合理的，那么在家长们意识中，与惩罚相反的就是某种放任。也就是说，如果惩罚没有作用，当孩子的言行与我们的价值观不一致时，我们就要放任不管。因此家长们只能认为："如果不惩罚，我就是放弃了自己的价值观，让孩子想干什么就干什么。"但正如下面我要探讨的，在放任不管，让人随心所欲、为所欲为，以及惩罚这类强制性手段之外，还有其他的处理方式。在此，我认为奖励和惩罚同样具有强制性。在这两种情况下，我们都是在对他人施加控制，并操纵外部环境，试图以此迫使他人的行为举止按照我们的喜好来。在这方面，奖励和惩罚出自同一种思维方式。

有一定品质的
连接

除了放任不管和使用强制性手段之外,还有一种办法,这要求我们能觉察以下两者之间微妙但却非常重要的区别——自己的目的是让他人按我们的意思去做(这是我不提倡的),还是创建一种有品质的连接,使每个人的需要都能得到满足。

我的经验是,无论我们沟通的对象是成人还是孩子,如果我们能认识到这两种目的之间的不同,我们就会有意识地不去尝试让他人按我们的意思去做,而是尝试创建一种彼此关心、相互尊重的有品质连接。在这样一种连接里,双方明白彼此的需要都很重要,同时他们也清楚,他们的需要和对方的幸福是互相依存的。不可思议的是,看似无法解决的冲突,就这样轻易化解了。

在解决与孩子的分歧时,是用强制性手段,还是创建有品质的连接，以便每个人的需要都得到满足，沟通方式是完全不同的。后者要求，把对孩子的道德评判，诸如对错、好坏等，转换成一种基于需要的语言。我们要告诉孩子，他们的行为与我们的需要一致，还是冲突，并且避免让他们感到愧疚和羞惭。这或许需要我们对孩子这样表达，"看到你打你兄弟，我吓坏了，因为我需要家里人都是安全的"，而不是"打你兄弟是错的"。或者，将"你也不把自己房间收拾干净，你可真懒"，换成"看到床没收拾好，我感到很沮丧，因为在保持家里整洁方面，我真的很需要支持"。

对于我们这些被老师和父母教育以道德评判的方式来思考的人，不去评判孩子行为的对错、好坏，而是基于需要进行表达，这种语言表达上的转化并不容易。另外，这样的表达也需要我们具备一种能力——当孩子们处于痛苦中时，我们能够临在陪伴他们，能够带着同理心去倾听他们。当我们被教育要做介入其中、给建议和解决问题的家长时，这同样不容易做到。

给家长们做培训时，我们会留意当孩子说"没人喜欢我"这类话时可能出现的状况。当一个孩子说出类似的话时，我相信，他/她是需要同理连接的，也就是基于尊重的理解，这能让孩子感受到，我们是和他/她在一起的，并且真正听到了他/她的感受和需要。有时我们可以静默倾听，用眼神表达我们与他们难过的感受在一起，与他们想和朋友更好地连接的需要在一起；又或者，也可以这样大声说出来："所以，听起来你真的挺难过的，因为你和朋友们在一起时没感受到多少乐趣。"

但是，很多家长认为，身为家长就要让孩子一直开心，所以一听到孩子这样表达，就会立刻介入，说些类似这样的话："那你看看，你是否做了什么可能让朋友疏远你的事？"或者反驳孩子："不是这样的，之前你有朋友，我敢肯定，你会交到更多朋友的。"或者给建议："也许你换种方式和朋友聊天，他们会更喜欢你。"

他们没有意识到,当一个人身处痛苦之中,需要的是临在陪伴和同理心。他们可能想要得到建议,但要在他们获得同理连接之后。我的孩子费了好一番功夫才教会我:"爸爸,在你收到我们手写的、非常正式的请求之前,不要给建议。"

奖励的局限

很多人相信使用奖励比使用惩罚更人性化，但这两者我都视为对他人的控制。而非暴力沟通，是基于与他人的合作。与他人合作时我们尝试影响对方，但方式并不是：不照我们的意思做就会受到惩罚，反之则得到奖励。这种影响力基于彼此的信任和尊重，能够使大家坦诚地相互倾听、相互学习，也能够使大家欣然地为他人付出。这种付出，来自为他人的幸福做出贡献的渴望，而不是出于对惩罚的恐惧，或是对奖励的期待。

要拥有这种与他人合作的能力，就需要坦诚沟通我们的感受和需要，且对对方没有任何形式的评判。要做到这一点，我们就要以恰当的方式告诉他人我们希望他们怎么做，这种方式不应被认为是要求或威胁。而且正如我所说，这还需要听到对方真正想要表达的感受和需要，并反馈准确的理解，而不是一下就介入其中，给出建议，或试图解决问题。

对于很多家长来说，我所谈论的沟通方式是如此不同，以至于他们会说："这么表达听起来很不自然。"恰好，我读到了一些甘地写的东西，其中他这样表达："不要混淆什么是自然的，什么是习惯的。"甘地经常提到，我们被教育的沟通和行事方式都是相当不自然的，但却已经成了习惯。在我们的文化中，出于各种各样的原因，我们已经被教育这样做，并且已经习惯这样做了。关于如何与孩子沟通，就我所受的教育来说，这话真是太对了。我被教育与孩子这样进行沟通——评判对错、好坏，使用惩罚，而这样的沟通方式被广泛地使用，作为家长，我很容易就对此习惯了。但我不会说，因为某件事已经成了习惯，它就是自然的。

我认识到，比起使用惩罚、奖励，或指责、羞辱作为强制性手段，以爱和尊重的方式与他人连接，使他们出于喜悦为他人做事，是更自然的方式。但这样的一种转化，需要大量的觉察和努力。

转变惯性的
沟通方式

记得有一次,我正从用习惯了的、评判式的沟通方式,向我现在所提倡的沟通方式转化。那天,我和大儿子之间起了冲突。我花了很长时间以我选择的方式跟他沟通,而不是用已经习惯了的方式。差不多所有第一时间出现在我头脑里的,都是对他所作所为进行评判的强制性表述。因此,我不得不停下,深呼吸,思考怎样才能和我的需要有更多连接,怎样才能和他的需要有更多连接。这花了我一些时间,而他则开始感到不耐烦,因为有个朋友正在外面等他,于是他说:"爸爸,你怎么花了这么长的时间来思考,你到底要说什么?"而我回答:"让我告诉你,被我压在嗓子眼儿,差点儿脱口而出的是什么:'照我说的做,否则我就踢你屁股。'"于是他说:"慢慢想,爸爸,慢慢想。"

因此,当事情与自己的价值观不那么一致时,我和孩子的沟通更倾向于慢慢来，从我选择的沟通方式出发，而不是用被教育的方式习惯性地回应。不幸的是，相比以尊重的方式对待孩子，我们常常会从周围人那里得到更多强烈的暗示，以惩罚的、评判的方式对待孩子。

记得有一年的感恩节晚餐，我竭尽所能以自己倡导的方式与小儿子沟通。这并不容易，因为他就要突破我的极限了。但我慢下来，深呼吸，尝试理解他的需要是什么，尝试理解我的需要是什么，这样我就可以以一种尊重的方式来表达了。有一位被教育以不同方式沟通的家族成员，观察着我与儿子的对话，某一刻，他凑过来在我耳边嘀咕道："如果这是我孩子，他会为他所说的话后悔的。"

我和很多有类似经历的家长交谈过，当他们试图与孩子建立更人性化的关系时，得到的往往是批评而不是支持。人们常常将我所说的误认为放任不管，或是不为孩子提供他们所需要的指导，却没理解实际上这是一种

"另类"的指导。这种指导基于对彼此信任,而不是一方将自己的权威强加给另一方。

目的是让孩子按我们的意思去做,而不是让每个人都得到自己想要的。最糟糕的结果,就是最终无论我们说什么,孩子都会听成是要求。而一旦人们听到要求,他们就很难注意到被请求的事的意义所在,因为,正如我之前说的,这威胁到了他们的自主权,对此每个人都有强烈的需求。人们希望做某事是出于自己的选择,而不是出于被迫。一旦人们听到"要求"的字眼,那么,让每个人的需要都得到满足的解决方案就很难出现了。

"家务战争"

我的孩子们被分配了不同的家务。举例来说，我最小的儿子，布雷特，那时 12 岁，被要求每周扔两次垃圾，以便垃圾清理人员可以将其收走。这是件挺简单的事，把垃圾从厨房水槽下面拿出来，拿到外面放在前院的草坪上，在那里垃圾会被收走。整个过程 5 分钟就可以完成，但每周两次需要扔垃圾的时候都会爆发战争。

那么，战争是如何开始的呢？通常我一叫他的名字就开始了。我大喊："布雷特。"当然，从我说话的语气他就能判断我已经生气了，因为我已断定他没有做他该做的事。即使我用两个街区外的邻居都能听到的声音大吼他的名字，他依然会做一些事让战争继续升级，是什么呢？他假装听不见，尽管他就在隔壁房间。我又会怎么做呢？我当然是更生气了，我也进一步升级，用比刚才更大的声音叫他，直到他再也不能假装听不见。而他会怎么做呢？他会问："你想干什么？"我说："垃圾没拿出去。"他说："你的观察力很强啊。"我说："拿出去。"他说："我会的，等会儿。"我说："上次你也是这么说的，但是你没有拿出去。"他说："那不代表这次我也不拿。"

就这么一个简单的扔垃圾的事儿，看看我们花费了多少精力。这件事在我们之间引发的紧张，全部来自那一刻我头脑里的想法：做这件事是他的责任，他应该做到，让他学习负起责任来是必要的。换句话说，这件事对他来说就是一个要求。

如果觉得不完成这项任务就会被惩罚或者被指责，人们就会把请求当作要求。一旦人们有这样的想法，做任何事情都不会有乐趣了。

我渐渐开始意识到这一点。我开始意识到，认为自己知道什么是正确的，认为自己作为家长的任务就是要让孩子规矩听话，这样的思维方式是多么有害。所以，有天晚上我和布雷特谈了为什么不倒垃圾这件事，这次，我学着更好地倾听，倾听他不照我的意思去做这件事背后的感受和需要。我如此清楚地看到，他有一个需要，那就是出于自己的选择做某事，而不是仅仅因为他不得不做。

当我发现这一点，我问他："布雷特，咱们怎么解决这个问题呢？我知道，过去我让你做什么而你却不做时，我心中就会升起评判，认为你是一个不肯合作的家庭成员，在这样的情况下，我的确就会要求你。咱们怎么才能从这样的过去中走出来，怎么才能到达一种出于其他动力驱使而不是被迫来为彼此做事的境地呢？"他提出了一个非常有帮助的办法。他说："爸爸，这样好不好，如果我不确定这是一个请求还是一个要求，我就问问你：'这是一个请求还是一个要求？'"我说："嘿，我喜欢这个主意，如果某件事情可以满足我的需要，但却与你的需要有冲突，我希望能听到这样的话，这样我们就可以找出一个让大家的需要都得到满足的办法。"

我喜欢他的建议，可以让我停下来看看头脑里正在上演怎样的假想。第二天他去上学前，我们有三次机会来试用这个建议，因为一早上我有三次叫他去做什么事情。每次他都看着我问："爸爸，这是一个请求还是一个要求？"而每次我审视内心，都发现那依旧是一个要求。我心里还是认为他就应该做某件事，那对他来说是唯一明智的选择。我已经做好准备，如果他不做，我就进一步更加强硬。因此，他这样提醒我是很有帮助的。每次我都停下来，连接自己的需要，并尝试理解他的需要，之后我对他说："好的，谢谢你，这很管用，之前是个要求，现在是请求了。"而他也能感受到我的内在发生了变化，这三次他都毫无异议地按我的请求做了。

无条件的爱

记得几年前,那时布雷特3岁,有一次我想知道自己是否向他和我的其他孩子们传达了一种无条件的爱。正当我思考这件事时,布雷特朝我走过来,他走进客厅,于是我问他:"布雷特,爸爸为什么爱你?"他看着我立刻说道:"是因为我现在把便壶放到厕所了吗?"听到他这样回答我非常难过。是啊,他怎么可能不这样认为呢?因为孩子们按我说的做,或是没按我说的做,我给出的回应是多么的不一样啊!

于是我对他说:"好吧,你这样做我真的很高兴,但那不是我爱你的原因。"然后他问:"那就是因为我不再往地板上扔食物了吧?"他这么说是因为前一天晚上他往地上扔食物时,我们之间发生了小争吵。我回答道:"你把食物放在盘子里,我同样很高兴,但那也不是我爱你的原因。"

这时他变得认真起来,看着我问道:"那,你到底为什么爱我呢,爸爸?"这下我开始琢磨,为什么自己要跟一个3岁的孩子谈"无条件的爱"这么抽象的话题呢?该如何对这么小的孩子表达呢?我脱口而出:"我爱你,就只是因为你是你。"说完我立即觉得,这解释真是既老套又含糊,但是他却懂了,他理解了我的意思,我从他的表情中看到了这点。

他高兴起来,看着我说:"哦,你爱我就只是因为我是我,爸爸,你爱我就只是因为我是我。"在接下来的两天里,几乎每十分钟他就会跑过来一次,用力拉着我,仰起头看着我说:"你爱我就只是因为我是我,爸爸,你爱我就只是因为我是我。"

以这样无条件的爱、尊重和接纳与他人沟通,不意味着我们要喜欢他人的行为,不意味着我们要纵容他人,并放弃我们自己的需要和价值观。这需要的是,无论他人按我们说的做，还是不按我们说的做，我们都给出同等的尊重。如果我们给出基于同理心的尊重，慢下来去理解为什么他们不按我们的意思去做，我们就可以继续思考，如何才能影响他人，让他人愿意做我们请求他们做的事。在某些情况下，当他人的行为严重威胁到我们的需要或安全，且缺乏沟通的时间或能力时，我们甚至可以使用强制手段。

不过，无条件的爱需要的是，无论人们的行为如何，他们都相信可以从我们这里得到具有一定品质的理解。

让我们的孩子做好准备

当然，我们的孩子经常身处的情境是缺乏这种无条件的接纳、尊重和爱的。比如可能是学校，老师们基于其他的思维方式而行使某种形式的权威，也就是说，尊重和爱不是无条件的，如果没按要求守规矩听话，就该受到惩罚或被指责。因此，作为家长的任务之一，就是向孩子展示保持人性的方式，即便周围人都在使用强制手段也要坚持这样做。

我作为家长，最幸福的日子之一，是大儿子去家附近的一所学校上学。那时他 12 岁。之前 6 年他都在另一所学校学习，而我在那里协助培训老师。那所学校以非暴力沟通的原则为基础。在那里，人们做某事不是出于会受到惩罚或奖励，而是他们明白这样做能够对自己和他人的幸福做出怎样的贡献。那里的价值体系是需要和请求，而非评判。在这样的学校学习了 6 年后，转到家附近的学校对他来说将会是一段十分不同的经历。令人沮丧的是,家附近这所学校并不是以一种我喜欢的方式在运行。

为什么这所学校老师的沟通方式和行为方式会不一样,在他去学校之前,我试着向他传达了一些我对这个问题的理解,并教给他一些应对可能发生的情况的技巧。他第一天放学回家,我就高兴地发现他已经用上了我教他的东西。

我问他:"里克,新学校怎么样?"他答道:"哦,还可以,爸爸。但是天啊,有些老师……"我能看出他感到苦恼,便问道:"怎么了?"

他说:"爸爸,我还没跨进教室门半步,真的,我正准备要进去的时候,这个男老师看见了我,一下冲过来对我大嚷道:'天哪,天哪,看这个小姑娘!'"这位老师之所以有这种反应,是因为我儿子那时留着长发,齐肩。以这位老师的思维方式，他显然觉得自己是一个能够评判对错的权威。关于应该留多长的头发这个问题是有标准答案的，如果有人没按标准来，那就必须指责他们，让他们愧疚，或者惩罚他们，以便他们改正。

听到孩子一到新学校就被这样"迎接"，我感到很难过，我说："你是怎么做的呢？"他答道："爸爸，我想起了你说的话——身处这种环境时，永远不要把决定自己服从或反抗的权力交由他人。"好吧，我很高兴他在那种情境下还能记住如此抽象的原则。我告诉他我很高兴他记得，然后又问："那你是怎么处理这个情况的呢？"

他答道："爸爸，我也是照你的建议处理的——如果有人用这样的方式跟我说话，尝试倾听他们的感受和需要，而不要把这当作是针对我个人的。所以我只是去尝试倾听他们的感受和需要。"我说："哇，真高兴你能想到这么做。那么你听到了什么呢？"

他说:"爸爸,这很明显,我听到他被惹恼了,他想要我剪掉自己的头发。""哦,"我说,"以这样的方式去理解他想表达的意思,你有什么感受?"他答道:"爸爸,我真为他感到难过,他秃顶,看起来还挺为头发烦恼的。"

"船长"游戏

在我的三个孩子分别3岁、4岁、7岁大时,我与他们有一段非常美好的经历。那时,我正在为老师们写一本书,关于如何建立这样一所学校——它的教育理念与非暴力沟通的原则相一致,与师生彼此尊重的原则相一致,注重培育自主权,也注重培育相互依存的价值观。作为建立这种学校的研究的一部分,我正打算更多地了解什么样的选择是孩子们自己就能做的,我们可以放心地将这些决定交给孩子们去做,这样他们就可以更好地锻炼自己在今后的人生中做选择的能力。

这时,我想到一个做这项研究的好办法,可以和我的孩子们一起玩一个我们称之为"船长"的游戏。在这个游戏里,每天我都会任命一个孩子做"船长"。轮到谁做"船长",我就会把很多通常由我来做的决定交由"船长"来做。但是,除非我已经做好准备,无论他们如何决定我都接受，否则我不会把某件事的决定权交给孩子。正如我所说，在这个游戏中，我的目的是了解孩子们如何做出选择，他们多久可以做出确定的选择，以及哪些选择对他们来说是有难度的。

我举个例子来说明这个游戏是如何进行的，以及对我来说这是一次多么好的学习经历。有一次，我带孩子们去干洗店取洗好的衣服。付钱的时候，干洗店的女士递给我三块糖给孩子们吃，我立即意识到这是个把决定权交给"船长"的好机会。于是，当她把糖递给我时，我说："呃，可以请你把糖给'船长'吗？"

当然，她不明白我在说什么，但是"船长"明白。3岁大的布雷特走过来，伸出手，女士把糖放在了他手里。然后我问："船长，可以请你来决定拿这些糖怎么办吗？"

好了，现在想象一下，对于这位3岁大的"船长"来说，这是一个多么艰难的决定。他站在那儿，手里有

3块糖，他有个姐姐正看着他，他还有个哥哥正看着他，他如何做出决定呢？经过认真考虑后，他把一块糖给了他哥哥，另一块给了他姐姐，自己吃了剩下的一块。

当我第一次告诉家长们这个故事时，其中一位家长说："好吧，不错，但那是因为你教过他们分享才是正确的。"我对那位家长说："哦，不那么准确。我这么说是因为一周前，在一个非常类似的情境下，他自己吃掉了全部3块糖。你能猜到第二天他遭遇了什么吗？是的，第二天他学到了，如果我们不考虑他人的需要，我们自己的需要也永远无法真正得到满足。他真的很快就学会了相互依存这一课。对他人的需要给予同等的关心，否则我们就永远无法真正照顾到我们自己。当孩子们可以真正自己来做决定时，他们那么快就明白了这一点，这真的让我挺激动的。"

正如我之前所说，让家长们放弃惩罚的观念并不容易。惩罚是必要的，这种观念在许多家长那里是根深蒂固的。如果孩子的行为可能伤害到自己或他人,他们想象不出除了惩罚还能怎么办。在纵容、放任不管,或使用某种惩罚措施之外,他们想不出还有什么其他选择。

强制手段的使用

我发现有一点很重要，那就是，让这些家长（即持"惩罚很必要"观点的家长）理解什么是出于保护目的而使用强制手段，以及让他们明白出于保护目的而使用强制手段与出于惩罚目的而使用强制手段这两者间的不同。那么，在什么情况下，我们必须对孩子使用某种形式的强制手段呢？

需要使用强制手段的情况是，没时间沟通，且孩子的行为可能会伤害到他们自己或其他人；或者也可能是对方没有交谈的意愿。因此，如果一个人不愿意交谈，或者当时没时间交谈，与此同时，他们的行为与我们的某个需要（比如保护他们）冲突，那么，我们可能就必须使用强制手段。但是我们必须要清楚，是出于保护目的，还是出于惩罚目的而使用强制手段，主要取决于使用强制手段的人的思维方式。

出于惩罚目的使用强制手段时，使用者对他人进行了道德评判，这种评判意味着某种错误理应受到惩罚。他人理应为自己的所作所为吃苦头，这就是惩罚的全部含义。支持这一观点的理论是：人类本性是有罪的、邪恶的，而纠正的方式就是令其悔过。我们要让他人知道，其行为多么令人厌恶，若要悔过就必须接受某种形式的惩罚，有时是打屁股这类体罚，有时是心理上的惩罚，比如通过某种方式让他人感到内疚或羞愧，从而厌恶自己。

出于保护目的使用强制手段，其背后的思维方式截然不同。在整个过程中不会有任何人被评判为坏人，或理应受到惩罚。我们的觉察全部集中在自己的需要上。我们注意到自己的什么需要受到了威胁，但不会以任何形式暗示孩子行为恶劣或犯了错误。

除了思维方式，出于保护目的与出于惩罚目的使用强制手段之间还有一个显著的区别，即使用强制手段的意图。出于惩罚目的使用强制手段，我们的意图是给对方制造痛苦和折磨，以使他们为其所作所为而惭愧。而出于保护目的使用强制手段，我们的意图就只是保护。我们为了保护自己的需要，在必要时会使用强制手段，事后，会进行必要的沟通来教导对方。

与此相关的一个例子就是当我的孩子们年纪还小时，我们住在一条繁华的街边。他们似乎会被街对面发生的一切深深吸引，但尚未理解突然冲到街上会给自己带来怎样的危险。我确信，如果能够就此问题进行充分的交流探讨，我是可以教导他们小心行事的，但同时我又担心，还没等我教导成功他们就因此丧命了。这就是一个出于保护目的而必须使用强制手段的情况，即在严重的事故发生之前，没时间对此进行沟通。所以，我是这样对他们说的："如果我看到你们跑到街上去，我就会把你们带去后院，在那里我不用担心你们被车撞到。"刚说完不久，其中一个孩子就忘了，开始往街上跑。我把他拎起来，带到后院放下，让他留在那里。这并不是一种惩罚，后院里能玩的特别多，那里有秋千和滑梯。我并没有试图让他吃苦头，只是要控制客观环境，以便我对安全的需要得到满足。

这时就会有许多家长问："虽然你说这不是惩罚，但孩子很有可能把这视为惩罚啊，难道不是吗？"是的，如果你曾用这种方法惩罚过孩子，或者孩子曾多次见过他人这样被惩罚，那么他们确实可能会将此视为惩罚。然而，最重要的是我们——父母们——对其中的区别保有意识，并确定自己使用强制手段时，目的是保护而不是惩罚。

要记住，出于保护目的而使用强制手段，关键是看到控制孩子和控制客观环境之间的差异。出于惩罚目的使用强制手段时，往往会通过使孩子对其所作所为感觉糟糕，而让他们对自己的行为产生一种发自内心的羞耻感、内疚，或恐惧，从而对孩子的行为进行控制。

出于保护目的使用强制手段，我们的意图不是控制孩子，而是控制客观环境，以便保护我们的需要，直到能够与对方进行十分必要的、有品质的沟通。这就好像我们给房子装上纱窗，以避免蚊虫叮咬，这就是出于保护目的使用强制手段。我们通过控制客观环境来阻止那些我们不愿意让它发生的事情。

互助社群

我在这里所倡导的养育方式，与大部分家长所采取的养育方式不同。在惩罚如此普遍的社会，考虑一种完全不同的选择是件挺困难的事。在这样的环境下，如果不对孩子做出惩罚或其他强制形式的家长行为，你就很容易遭到误解。加入一个互助社群会对你有极大的帮助。这样的社群理解我所阐述的养育理念，在这里，人们会得到这个社会通常不会给予的支持，这有助于你继续坚持实践这种理念。

作为家长多么艰难，跌回旧有模式多么容易，因此，如果能时常从一个互助社群中获得大量的同理心，我确定自己能更好地保持我所倡导的状态。得知其他家长也尝试像我这样与他们的孩子建立连接，我们相互交谈，彼此倾听，无论是对方的成功还是挫败感，都将给我们带来莫大的支持。我也注意到，我加入这类社群之后，即使在非常困难的情境下，也能与孩子保持这种有品质的连接。

女儿还很小的时候，我从她那里收获了一个启示，这是我倡导该养育方式得到的鼓舞人心的巨大回报之一。那是一个星期日的早上，一周中我唯一可以休息的、对我来说非常宝贵的时段。

在那个特别的星期日早上，一对夫妻打电话给我，询问是否可以见面为他们做咨询。他们的关系处于危机中，希望我能帮助他们。我同意了，没有好好审视自己的内心——我的需要是什么，我多么不满对方侵占了自己放松的时间。当我在客厅为他们做咨询时，门铃响了，警察又给我带来了一位需要接待的年轻女士，我之前曾为她做过咨询。这次，警察发现她时，她正坐在铁轨上——她就是通过这种方式来表达她想见我的意愿的。她太胆怯了，以至于不敢再次打电话约我，只好坐在铁轨上来表达她的痛苦。她比镇上任何一个人都更清楚火车时刻表,因此确定警察会在火车撞到她之前将她带离。

然后警察离开了,把烂摊子留给了我——有位年轻的女士在厨房哭泣,还有对不和的夫妻在客厅,我两边奔波,试图亲切地为他们双方做咨询。当我做这些的时候——在两个房间来回穿梭、看手表、希望这之后还能有点儿时间留给自己——楼上的三个孩子打了起来。我三步两步奔上楼去,发现了一些有趣至极的事儿。也许某天我会将这一点整理记录到一篇学术论文中去:海拔对疯狂行为的影响。因为你看,在楼下我是个十分亲切的人,给这对夫妇关怀,也给另一个房间的年轻女士关怀,但是上了一层楼我就陷入了疯狂。

我对孩子们说道:"你们怎么回事?看不见我正在楼下接待伤心痛苦的人们吗?现在回你们的房间去!"于是他们都回到各自的房间,摔上门,声音大到我都不敢相信那是摔门声。听到第一声摔门声,我更加愤怒了,而第二声让我比第一声还要愤怒。但幸运的是，听到第三声，不知为什么，我反倒发觉了此情此景的幽默之处——我对楼下的人们多么容易给予亲切关怀，而对于楼上的家人们，却是多么快速地转变为粗暴的态度。

我深吸一口气，首先走进了大儿子的房间，告诉他我为自己冲他发脾气而感到难过，恐怕实际上我是对楼下的人有情绪。他理解了，回答道："没事儿的，爸爸，没什么大不了的。"我又走进小儿子的房间，从他那里得到了非常类似的回答。接着，我走进女儿的房间，告诉她我为自己对她说话的方式感到难过，她走过来，把头靠在我的肩膀上说："没事儿的，爸爸，没有人是完美的。"

多么珍贵的提醒啊！是的，我的孩子们喜欢我的这种努力——以关切的、充满爱和同情心的、有同理心的方式与他们连接。但是，他们也能理解人性的弱点，知道有时候我这样做有多么难，这是多么慰藉人心的理解啊。

所以在最后，我将女儿给我的、令人感到宽慰的建议提供给大家——没有人是完美的。记住，任何值得做的事，即使做得不够好，也依然值得去做。养育这件事，毋庸置疑，是非常值得做的，但有时我们也会做得不够好。如果我们因为自己不是完美的父母而对自己态度粗暴，那么受苦的将是我们的孩子。

我常对来参加工作坊的家长们说，地狱就是，有孩子，并且认为存在"完美好家长"这么一回事儿。这种想法意味着，每当我们不够完美时，我们就会责怪和抨击自己，而我们的孩子却不会从中受益。所以，我不建议把成为完美的家长作为目标，而是建议把逐渐成为少一些愚笨的家长作为目标——从每次没能给孩子他们所需要的理解中学习，从每次我们没能真诚地表达自己的需要中学习。在我的经验里，为了给予孩子他们所需要的，作为父母是需要得到情感支持的，而我们并未得到。

我们能真正以一种关切的方式给出多大程度的爱与理解，取决于我们自己获得了多大程度的类似的爱与理解。这就是为什么我强烈建议父母们考虑，在我们的朋友和周围人中间为自己创建一个互助社群，他们能够以对我们彼此都有益的形式，给予我们需要向孩子给出的理解。

希望我以上所说的某些内容，可以帮助你成长、越来越接近自己想要成为的家长。

非暴力沟通的四个步骤

清楚地、不带指责或批评地表达我是怎样的	同理接收你是怎样的,而不是听到指责或批评

1. 观察

我所观察到的(看到的、听到的、记得的、不带评判地想象的)是否为我的健康和幸福做出了贡献: "当我(看,听)……"	你所观察到的(看到的、听到的、记得的、不带评判地想象的)是否为你的健康和幸福做出了贡献: "当你(看,听)……" (有时会以静默的方式同理倾听。)

2. 感受

和我的观察相关的感受(情绪、感觉而不是想法) "我感到……"	和你的观察相关的感受(情绪、感觉而不是想法) "你感到……"

3. 需要

引发我的感受的根源是我需要或看重的（而不是偏好的或特定的）行为：	引发你的感受的根源是你需要或看重的（而不是偏好的或特定的）行为：
"……因为我需要/看重……"	"……因为你需要/看重……"

为了服务我的生命需要，清晰地表达请求而不是要求。	同理倾听什么请求能服务你的生命需要，而不是听到任何要求。

4. 请求

我想让对方采取的具体行动是：	对方想采取的具体行动是：
"你愿意试试……吗？"	"你愿意……吗？" （有时会以静默的方式同理倾听。）

人类共有的一些基本感受

当需要得到满足时

○ 惊奇　　　○ 舒适　　○ 自信　　○ 期待
○ 精力充沛　○ 满足　　○ 开心　　○ 满怀希望
○ 受启发的　○ 好奇　　○ 愉快　　○ 感动
○ 乐观　　　○ 自豪　　○ 放心　　○ 兴奋
○ 惊喜　　　○ 感激　　○ 触动　　○ 信赖

当需要没有得到满足时

○ 生气　○ 烦闷　　○ 担心　　○ 困惑
○ 失望　○ 沮丧　　○ 忧虑　　○ 尴尬
○ 气馁　○ 无助　　○ 绝望　　○ 焦躁
○ 恼怒　○ 孤单　　○ 紧张　　○ 不堪重负
○ 困惑　○ 不情愿　○ 悲伤　　○ 不安

人类共有的一些基本需要

自主性
- 选择梦想、目标、价值
- 选择实现梦想、目标和价值的方法

庆祝 / 哀悼
- 庆祝生命的创造和梦想的实现
- 哀悼失去：亲人离世、梦想破灭等

一致性
- 真实
- 创造
- 意义
- 自我价值

生理需要
- 空气
- 食物
- 运动锻炼
- 保护生命免受病毒、细菌、害虫、食肉动物等的伤害
- 休息
- 性表达
- 住所
- 身体接触

- 水

玩耍

- 乐趣
- 快乐

精神需要

- 美
- 和谐
- 灵感
- 秩序
- 和平

相互依存

- 接纳
- 欣赏
- 亲密关系
- 社群
- 关心
- 服务生命
- 情绪安全
- 同理心
- 诚实（诚实的能力可以让我们从自身的局限中学习）
- 爱
- 肯定
- 尊重
- 支持
- 信任
- 理解

英文原版

Introduction
Raising Children Compassionately

I've been teaching Nonviolent Communication to parents for thirty years. I would like to share some of the things that have been helpful to me and to the parents that I've worked with, and to share with you some insights I've had into the wonderful and challenging occupation of parenting.

I'd first like to call your attention to the danger of the word "child," if we allow it to apply a different quality of respect than we would give to someone who is not labeled a child. Let me show you what I am referring to.

In parent workshops that I've done over the years, I've often started by dividing the group into two. I put one group in one room, and the other in a different room, and I give each group the task of writing down on a large paper a dialogue between themselves and another person in a conflict situation. I tell both groups what the conflict is. The only difference is that I tell one group the other person is their child, and to the second group I say the other person is their neighbor.

Then we get back into a large group and we look at

these different sheets of paper outlining the dialogue that the groups would have, in the one case thinking that the other person was their child, and in the other case, the neighbor. (And incidentally, I haven't allowed the groups to discuss with the other group who the person was in their situation, so that both groups think that the situation is the same.)

After they've had a chance to scan the written dialogues of both groups, I ask them if they can see a difference in terms of the degree of respect and compassion that was demonstrated. Every time I've done this, the group that was working on the situation with the other person being a child was seen as being less respectful and compassionate in their communication than the group that saw the other person as a neighbor. This painfully reveals to the people in these groups how easy it is to dehumanize someone by the simple process of simply thinking of him or her as "our child."

My Own Awareness

I had an experience one day that really heightened my awareness of the danger of thinking of people as children.

This experience followed a weekend in which I had worked with two groups : a street gang and a police department. I was mediating between the two groups. There had been considerable violence between them, and they had asked that I serve in the role of a mediator. After spending as much time as I did with them, dealing with the violence they had toward one another, I was exhausted. And as I was driving home afterward, I told myself, I never want to be in the middle of another conflict for the rest of my life. And of course, when I walked in my back door, my three children were fighting. I expressed my pain to them in a way that we advocate in Nonviolent Communication. I expressed how I was feeling, what my needs were, and what my requests were. I did it this way. I shouted : "When I hear all of this going on right now, I feel extremely tense ! I have a real need for some peace and quiet after the weekend I've been through ! So would you all be willing to give me that time and space ? "

My oldest son looked at me and said, "Would you like to talk about it? " Now, at that moment, I dehumanized him in my thinking. Why ? Because I said to myself : "How cute. Here's a nine-year-old boy trying to help his father." But take a closer look at how I was disregarding his offer because of his age, because I had him labeled as a child. Fortunately I saw that this was going on in my head, and maybe I was able to see it more clearly because the work I had been doing between the street gang and the police showed me the danger of thinking of people in terms of labels instead of their humanness.

So instead of seeing him as a child and thinking to myself, "how cute," I saw a human being who was reaching out to another human being in pain, and I said out loud, "Yes, I would like to talk about it." And the three of them followed me into another room and listened while I opened up my heart to how painful it was to see that people could come to a point of wanting to hurt one another simply because they hadn't been trained to see the other person's humanness. After talking about it for forty-five minutes I felt wonderful, and as I recall we turned the stereo on and danced like fools for a while.

Our Education As Parents

So I'm not suggesting that we don't use words like "child" as a shorthand way of letting people know that we're talking about people of a certain age. I'm talking about when we allow labels like this to keep us from seeing the other person as a human being, in a way which leads us to dehumanize the other person because of the things our culture teaches us about "children." Let me show you an extension of what I'm talking about, how the label child can lead us to behave in a way that's quite unfortunate.

Having been educated, as I was, to think about parenting, I thought that it was the job of a parent to make children behave. You see, once you define yourself as an authority, a teacher or parent, in the culture that I was educated in, you then see it as your responsibility to make people that you label a "child" or a "student" behave in a certain way.

I now see what a self-defeating objective this is, because I have learned that any time it's our objective to get another person to behave in a certain way, people are likely to resist no matter what it is we're asking for. This seems to be true whether the otherperson is two or ninety-two years of age.

This objective of getting what we want from other people, or getting them to do what we want them to do, threatens the autonomy of people, their right to choose what they want to do. And whenever people feel that they're not free to choose what they want to do, they are likely to resist, even if they see the purpose in what we are asking and would ordinarily want to do it. So strong is our need to protect our autonomy, that if we see that someone has this single-mindedness of purpose, if they are acting like they think that they know what's best for us and are not leaving it to us to make the choice of how we behave, it stimulates our resistance.

The Limitations of Coercion and Punishment

I'll be forever grateful to my children for educating me about the limitations of the objective of getting other people to do what you want. They taught me that, first of all, I couldn't make them do what I want. I couldn't make them do anything. I couldn't make them put a toy back in the toy box. I couldn't make them make their bed. I couldn't make them eat. Now, that was quite a humbling lesson for me as a parent, to learn about my powerlessness, because somewhere I had gotten it into my mind that it was the job of a parent to make a child behave. And here were these young children teaching me this humbling lesson, that I couldn't make them do anything. All I could do is make them wish they had.

And whenever I would be foolish enough to do that, that is, to make them wish they had, they taught me a second lesson about parenting and power that has proven very valuable to me over the years. And that lesson was that anytime I would make them wish they had, they would make me wish I hadn't made them wish they had. Violence begets violence.

They taught me that any use of coercion on my part would invariably create resistance on their part, which could lead to an adversarial quality in the connection between us. I don't want to have that quality of connection with any human being, but especially not with my children, those human beings that I'm closest to and taking responsibility for. So my children are the last people that I want to get into these coercive games of which punishment is a part.

Now this concept of punishment is strongly advocated by most parents. Studies indicate that about 80 percent of American parents firmly believe in corporal punishment of children. This is about the same percentage of the population who believes in capital punishment of criminals. So with such a high percentage of the population believing that punishment is justified and necessary in the education of children, I've had plenty of opportunity over the years to discuss this issue with parents, and I'm pleased with how people can be helped to see the limitations of any kind of punishment, if they'll simply ask themselves two questions.

Question number one : What do you want the child to do differently ? If we ask only that question, it can certainly seem that punishment sometimes works, because certainly through the threat of punishment or application of punishment, we can at times influence a child to do what we would like the child to do.

However, when we add a second question, it has been my experience that parents see that punishment never works. The second question is: What do we want the child's reasons to be for acting as we would like them to act? It's that question that helps us to see that punishment not only doesn't work, but it gets in the way of our children doing things for reasons that we would like them to do things.

Since punishment is so frequently used and justified, parents can only imagine that the opposite of punishment is a kind of permissiveness in which we do nothing when children behave in ways that are not in harmony with our values. So therefore parents can think only, "If I don't punish, then I give up my own values and just allow the child to do whatever he or she wants." As I'll be discussing below, there are other approaches besides permissiveness, that is, just letting people do whatever they want to do, or coercive tactics such as punishment. And while I'm at it, I'd like to suggest that reward is just as coercive as punishment. In both cases we are using power over people, controlling the environment in a way that tries to force people to behave in ways that we like. In that respect, reward comes out of the same mode of thinking as punishment.

A Certain Quality of Connection

There is another approach besides doing nothing or using coercive tactics. It requires an awareness of the subtle but important difference between our objective being to get people to do what we want, which I'm not advocating, and instead being clear that our objective is to create the quality of connection necessary for everyone's needs to be met.

It has been my experience, whether we are communicating with children or adults, that when we see the difference between these two objectives, and we are consciously not trying to get a person to do what we want, but trying to create a quality of mutual concern, a quality of mutual respect, a quality where both parties think that their needs matter and they are conscious that their needs and the other person's well-being are interdependent—it is amazing how conflicts, which otherwise seem irresolvable, are easily resolved.

Now, this kind of communication that is involved in creating the quality of connection necessary for everybody's needs to get met is quite different from that communication used if we are using coercive forms of resolving differences with children. It requires a shift away from evaluating children in moralistic terms such as right/wrong, good/bad, to a language based on needs. We need to be able to tell children whether what they're doing is in harmony with our needs, or in conflict with our needs, but to do it in a way that doesn't stimulate guilt or shame on the child's part. So it might require our saying to the child, "I'm scared when I see you hitting your brother, because I have a need for people in the family to be safe," instead of, "It's wrong to hit your brother." Or it might require a shift away from saying, "You are lazy for not cleaning up your room," to saying, "I feel frustrated when I see that the bed isn't made, because I have a real need for support in keeping order in the house."

This shift in language away from classifying children's behavior in terms of right and wrong, and good and bad, to a language based on needs, is not easy for those of us who were educated by teachers and parents to think in moralistic judgments. It also requires an ability to be present to our children, and listen to them with empathy when they are in distress. This is not easy when we have been trained as parents to want to jump in and give advice, or to try to fix things.

So when I'm working with parents, we look at situations that are likely to arise where a child might say something like,"Nobody likes me." When a child says something like that, I believe the child needs an empathic kind of connection. And by that I mean a respectful understanding where the child feels that we are there and really hear what he or she is feeling and needing. Sometimes we can do this silently, just showing in our eyes that we are with their feelings of sadness, and their need for a different quality of connection with their friends. Or it could involve our saying out loud something like,"So it sounds like you're really feeling sad, because you aren't having very much fun with your friends."

But many parents, defining their role as requiring them to make their children happy all the time, jump in when a child says something like that, and say things like, "Well, have you looked at what you've been doing that might have been driving your friends away?" Or they disagree with the child, saying : "Well, that's not true. You've had friends in the past. I'm sure you'll get more friends." Or they give advice : "Maybe if you'd talk differently to your friends, your friends would like you more."

What they don't realize is that all human beings, when they're in pain, need presence and empathy. They may want advice, but they want that after they've received the empathic connection. My own children have taught me the hard way that, "Dad, please withhold all advice unless you receive a request in writing from us signed by a notary."

The Limitations of Rewards

Many people believe that it's more humane to use reward than punishment. But both of them I see as power over others, and Nonviolent Communication is based on power with people. And in power with people, we try to have influence not by how we can make people suffer if they don't do what we want, or how we can reward them if they do. It's a power based on mutual trust and respect, which makes people open to hearing one another and learning from one another, and to giving to one another willingly out of a desire to contribute to one another's well-being, rather than out of a fear of punishment or hope for a reward.

We get this kind of power, power with people, by being able to openly communicate our feelings and needs without in any way criticizing the other person. We do that by offering them what we would like from them in a way that is not heard as demanding or threatening. And as I have said, it also requires really hearing what other people are trying to communicate, showing an accurate understanding rather than quickly jumping in and giving advice, or trying to fix things.

For many parents, the way I'm talking about communicating is so different that they say, "Well, it just doesn't seem natural to communicate that way." At just the right time, I read something that Gandhi had written in which he said, "Don't mix up that which is habitual with that which is natural." Gandhi said that very often we've been trained to communicate and act in ways that are quite unnatural, but they are habitual in the sense that we have been trained for various reasons to do it that way in our culture. And that certainly rang true to me in the way that I was trained to communicate with children. The way I was trained to communicate by judging rightness and wrongness, goodness and badness, and the use of punishment was widely used and very easily became habitual for me as a parent. But I wouldn't say that because something is habitual that it is natural.

I learned that it is much more natural for people to connect in a loving, respectful way, and to do things out of joy for one another, rather than using punishment and reward or blame and guilt as means of coercion. But such a transformation does require a good deal of consciousness and effort.

Transforming Your Habitual Communication

I can recall one time when I was transforming myself from a habitually judgmental way of communicating with my children to the way that I am now advocating. On the day I'm thinking of, my oldest son and I were having a conflict, and it was taking me quite awhile to communicate it in the way that I was choosing to, rather than the way that had become habitual. Almost everything that came into my mind originally was some coercive statement in the form of a judgment of him for saying what he did. So I had to stop and take a deep breath, and think of how to get more in touch with my needs, and how to get more in touch with his needs. And this was taking me awhile. And he was getting frustrated because he had a friend waiting for him outside, and he said, "Daddy, it's taking you so long to talk." And I said, "Let me tell you what I can say quickly: Do it my way or I'll kick your butt." He said: "Take your time, Dad. Take your time."

So yes, I would rather take my time and come from an energy that I choose in communicating with my children, rather than habitually responding in a way that I have been trained to do, when it's not really in harmony with my own values. Sadly, we will often get much more reinforcement from those around us for behaving in a punitive, judgmental way, than in a way that is respectful to our children.

I can recall one Thanksgiving dinner when I was doing my best to communicate with my youngest son in the way that I am advocating, and it was not easy, because he was testing me to the limits. But I was taking my time, taking deep breaths, trying to understand what his needs were, trying to understand my own needs so I could express them in a respectful way. Another member of the family, observing my conversation with my son, but who had been trained in a different way of communicating, reached over at one point and whispered in my ear,"If that was my child, he'd be sorry for what he was saying."

I've talked to a lot of other parents who have had similar experiences who, when they are trying to relate in more human ways with their own children, instead of getting support, often get criticized. People can often mistake what I'm talking about as permissiveness or not giving children the direction they need, instead of understanding that it's a different quality of direction. It's a direction that comes from two parties trusting each other, rather than one party forcing his or her authority on another.

One of the most unfortunate results of making our objective to get our children to do what we want, rather than having our objective be for all of us to get what we want, is that eventually our children will be hearing a demand in whatever we are asking. And whenever people hear a demand, it's hard for them to keep focus on the value of whatever is being requested, because, as I said earlier, it threatens their autonomy, and that's a strong need that all people have. They want to be able to do something when they choose to do it, and not because they are forced to do it. As soon as a person hears a demand, it's going to make any resolution that will get everybody's needs met much harder to come by.

"Chore Wars"

For example, my children were given different tasks to do around the house. My youngest son, Brett, then twelve, was being asked to take the garbage out, twice a week, so that it could be picked up by the garbage removal people.

This involved a simple act of removing the garbage from underneath the kitchen sink, and taking it out on the front lawn where it could be picked up. This whole process could be done in five minutes. But it created a battle twice a week when the garbage was to go out.

Now, how did this battle start? It usually started with my simply mentioning his name. I would say, "Brett." But of course, the way I said it he could pick up that I was already angry because I was judging him as not doing what he should do. And even though I was saying his name loud enough so that the neighbors two blocks down could hear it, what does he do to keep escalating the war? He pretends that he doesn't hear me, even though he's in the next room. Well, what do I do ? I get even angrier of course, and I escalate further, and now I say the name even louder the second time than the first time, so that even he can't pretend that he doesn't hear me. And what does he do ? He says,"What do you want ?" I say,"The garbage isn't out." He says, "You're very perceptive." And I say, "Get it out." And he says,"I will, later." And I say,"You said that last time but you didn't do it." And he says, "That doesn't mean I won't do it this time."

Look at all that energy going into the simple act of getting the garbage taken out. All the tension it creates between us, all because at that time I had it in my mind that it was his job to do it, that he should do it, that it was necessary for him to learn responsibility. So in other words, it was being presented to him as a demand.

People receive requests as demands if they think they will be punished or blamed if they don't do the task. When people have that idea, it takes all the joy out of doing anything.

One night I had a talk with Brett about this at a time when I was starting to get the point. I was starting to see how my thinking that I knew what was right, that my job as a parent was to get the children to behave, was destructive. So one night we had a talk about why the garbage wasn't going out, and by this time I was starting to learn how to listen better, to hear the feelings and needs that were behind his not doing what I asked.

And I saw so clearly that he had a need to do things because he chose to do them, and not to do them simply because he was being forced to do them.

So when I saw this, I said to him, Brett, how do we get out of this? I know I really have been making demands in the past in the sense that when you didn't do things I wanted you to do, I would make judgments of you as being not a cooperative member of the family. So how do we get out of this history that we have, and how do we get to a place where we can do things for each other out of a different kind of energy? And he came up with an idea that was very helpful. He said, "Dad, how about if I'm not sure if it's a request or a demand, I ask you, 'Is that a request or a demand?'" I said: "Hey, I like that idea. It would force me to really stop and look at my thinking, and really see whether I am actually saying,'Hey, I'd really like you to do this, it would meet my need, but if your needs are in conflict I'd like to hear that, and let's figure out a way to get everybody's needs met.'"

I liked his suggestion, to stop and really see what kind of assumptions were going on in me. And the next day, before he went to school, we had three chances to test this out. Because three times in the morning I asked him to do something, and each time he looked at me and said, "Dad, is that a request or a demand?" And each time I looked inside, I saw that it was still a demand. I still had this thinking in me that he should do it, that it was the only reasonable thing for him to do. I was prepared that if he didn't do it, to get progressively more coercive. So it was helpful that he called this to my attention. Each time I stopped, got in touch with my needs, tried to hear his needs, and I said to him: "OK, thank you. That helps. It was a demand, and now it's a request." And he could sense the difference in me. And each of those three times he did it without question.

When people hear demands, it looks to them as though our caring and respect and love are conditional. It looks as though we are only going to care for them as people when they do what we want.

Unconditional Love

I remember one time, years ago, when Brett was three

years old. I was wondering if I was communicating an unconditional quality of love to him and my other children as well. But he happened to be the one that came upon me at that time when I was thinking about this subject. As he came into the living room, I said, "Brett, why does Dad love you ? " He looked at me and immediately said, "Because I make my potties in the toilet now ?" I felt very sad the moment he said that because it was so clear, how could he think differently ? How differently I respond to my children when they do what I want, than when they don't do what I want.

So I said to him, "Well, I do appreciate that, but that's not why I love you." And then he said, "Well, because I don't throw my food on the floor anymore ? " He was referring there to a little disagreement we'd had the night before when he was throwing some food on the floor. And I said : "Well, here again, I do appreciate it when you keep your food on your plate. But that's not why I love you."

Now he gets very serious, and looks at me and says, "Well, why do you love me, daddy ? " And now I was wondering, why did I get into abstract conversation about unconditional love with a three-year-old? How do you express this to someone his age? And I blurted out, "Well, I just love you because you're you." At the time, the immediate thought I had was, that's pretty trite and vague, but he got it. He got the message. I just saw it in his face. He brightened up and he looked at me and he said: "Oh, you just love me because I'm me, daddy. You just love me because I'm me." The next two days it seemed like every ten minutes he was running over to me and pulling at my side and looking up and saying: "You just love me because I'm me, daddy. You just love me because I'm me."

So to communicate this quality of unconditional love, respect, acceptance to other people, this doesn't mean that we have to like what they're doing. It doesn't mean we have to be permissive and give up our needs or values. What it requires is that we show people the same quality of respect when they don't do what we ask, as when they do. After we have shown that quality of respect through empathy, through taking the time to understand why they didn't do what we would like, we can then pursue how we might influence them to willingly do what we ask. In some cases, where people are behaving in a serious way that threatens our needs or safety and there's not time or ability to communicate about it, we may even use force.

But unconditional love requires that no matter how people behave, they trust that they'll receive a certain quality of understanding from us.

Preparing Our Children

Now of course, our children are often going to be in situations where they're not going to receive this unconditional acceptance and respect and love. They're going to be in schools, perhaps, where the teachers are using a form of authority that's based on other ways of thinking, namely that you have to earn respect and love— that you deserve to be punished or blamed if you don't behave in a certain way. So one of our tasks as parents is to show our children a way of staying human, even when they are being exposed to others who are using a form of coercion.

One of my happiest days as a parent was when my

oldest son went off to a neighborhood school. He was twelve years old at the time. He had just finished six years in a school where I'd helped train the teachers, a school based on principles of Nonviolent Communication where people were expected to do things not because of punishment or reward, but because they saw how it was contributing to their own and other people's well-being, where evaluation was in terms of needs and requests, not in terms of judgments. So this was going to be quite a different experience for him after six years in such a school, to go to the neighborhood school, which I'm sad to say wasn't functioning in a way that I would have liked.

But before he had gone off to this school, I had tried to provide him with some understanding of why teachers in this school might be communicating and behaving in a different way, and I tried to provide him with some skills for handling that situation should it occur. When he came home from school the first day I was delighted to find out how he had used what I had offered him.

I asked him, "Rick, how was the new school？" And he said："Oh, it's OK, Dad. But boy, some of those teachers."I could see that he was distressed, and I said, "What happened ? "

He said : "Dad, I wasn't even halfway in the door, really I was just walking in, when this man teacher saw me and came running over and screamed at me, 'My, my, look at the little girl.'" Now, what that teacher was reacting to was, my son had long hair at the time, down to his shoulders. And this teacher had a way of thinking, apparently, where he thought he as the authority knew what was right, that there was a right way to wear hair, and that if somebody doesn't do things the right way, then you have to shame them or guilt them or punish them into doing it.

I felt sad to hear that my child would be greeted that way his first moment in the new school. And I said, "How did you handle it ? " And he said,"Dad, I remembered what you said, that when you're in a place like that, never to give them the power to make you submit or rebel." Well, I was delighted that he would remember that abstract principle at such a time. And I told him I was glad that he remembered it, and I said, "How did you handle the situation ? "

He said: "Dad, I also did what you suggested, that when people are talking to me that way, to try to hear what they're feeling and needing and not take it personally. Just to try to hear their feelings and needs." I said, "Wow, am I glad that you thought to do that. What did you hear?"

He said, "Dad, it was pretty obvious. I heard that he was irritated and wanted me to cut my hair." "Oh," I said, "how did that leave you feeling, to receive his message in that way?" And he said: "Dad, I felt really sad for the man. He was bald, and seemed to have a problem about hair."

The "Captain" Game

I had a very good experience with my children when they were three, four, and seven years old. I was then writing a book for teachers about how to create schools in harmony with principles of Nonviolent Communication, in harmony with principles of mutual respect between teachers and students, schools that fostered the values of autonomy and interdependence. And as part of the research I was doing in setting up these schools, I was wanting to learn more about what kind of choices we could trust children to make. And to be able to turn these decisions over to children so that they were better able to develop their ability to make choices in their lives.

At this time, I thought a good way of learning more about this might be to play a game with my children which we called Captain. In this game each day I would appoint one of the children as Captain. And when it was their turn as the Captain, I would turnover many decisions that I would usually make to the Captain to make. But I wouldn't give this decision to the child unless I was prepared to live with however they made the choice. As I said, my purpose in this game was to learn how children could make choices, how early they could make certain choices, and which ones might not be easy for them to make.

Here is an example of how this game went, and what a good learning experience it was for me. Once I took the children with me to pick up some dry cleaning, and as I paid, the woman started to hand me three pieces of candy for the children.Immediately I saw a good opportunity to turn a decision over to the Captain. As the woman handed me the candy, I said, "Uh, would you please give the candy to the Captain?"

Well, she didn't know what I was talking about, but the Captain did. Three-year-old Brett walked over, held out his hand, and she placed the candy in his hand. And then I said, "Captain, would you please choose what to do with this candy?"

Well, now imagine this rough decision for this three-year-old Captain. Here he is, three pieces of candy in his hand, he has a sister looking at him, he has a brother looking at him, how does he choose? Well, after a serious consideration, he gave one piece to his brother, and one piece to his sister, and he ate the other himself.

When I first told that story to a group of parents, one of the parents said, "Well, yes, but that's because you had taught him that it was right to share." And I said to the parent: "Oh, not accurate. I know that's not so, because a week before he was in a very similar situation, and he ate all three pieces of candy. Can you guess what happened to him the next day? Yes, he learned the next day that if we don't take other people's needs into consideration, that our own needs can never really be met. He really got a quick lesson on interdependence. It was thrilling for me to see how quickly children saw this when they really had choices to make. That we can never really take care of ourselves without showing equal concern for the needs of others."

As I said earlier, it's not easy for parents to let go of the concept of punishment. It's deeply ingrained in many parents that this is a necessity. And they can't imagine what else can be done when children are behaving in ways that might be harmful to themselves and other people. And they can't conceive of other options besides permissiveness, just letting it go, or using some kind of punitive action.

The Use of Force

I have found it very important to get across to such parents the concept of the protective use of force, and to get them to see the difference between the protective use of force and the punitive use of force. So when might we sometimes have to use a form of force with our children ?

Well, the conditions calling for this would be when there isn't time to communicate, and the child's behavior might be injurious to themselves or other people. Or it could be that the person isn't willing to talk. So if a person isn't willing to talk, or there isn't time to talk, and meanwhile they are behaving in a way that is conflict with one of our needs, such as a need to protect people, we might have to use force. But now we have to see the difference between the protective and the punitive use of force. And one way that these two uses of force differ is in the thinking of the person who is engaging in the force.

In the punitive use of force, the person using such force has made a moralistic judgment of the other person, a judgment that implies some kind of wrongness that is deserving of punishment. This person deserves to suffer for what they've done. That's the whole idea of punishment. It comes out of these ideas that human beings are basically sinful, evil creatures and the corrective process is to make them penitent. We have to get them to see how terrible they are for doing what they're doing. And the way we make them penitent is to use some form of punishment to make them suffer. Sometimes this can be a physical punishment in the form of spanking, or it could be a psychological punishment in the form of trying to make them hate themselves, through making them feel guilty or ashamed.

The thinking behind the protective use of force is radically different. There is no consciousness that the other person is bad or deserving of punishment. Our consciousness is fully focused on our needs. We are conscious of what need of ours is in danger. But we are not in any way implying badness or wrongness to the child.

So this kind of thinking is one significant difference between the protective use of force and the punitive use of force. And this thinking is closely related to a second difference, the intent. In the punitive use of force, it is our intent to create pain and suffering for the other person, to make them sorry for what they did. In the protective use of force, our intent is only to protect. We protect our needs, and then later we'll have the communication necessary to educate the person. But at the moment it may be necessary touse the force to protect.

An example of this would be, when my children were young, we lived on a busy street. And they seemed to be fascinated with what was going on across the street, and they hadn't yet learned the dangers of what can happen to you if you just dart out in the street. I was certain that if we could talk long enough about this, I could educate them, but in the meantime I was afraid that they could be killed. So here was a case for the protective use of force, there not being the time to communicate about this before something serious could happen. So what I said to them was, "If I see you running in the street, I'm going to put you in the backyard where I don't have to worry about you getting hit by a car." Not long after I said that, one of them forgot and started to run in the street. I picked him up, carried him into the yard and put him there, not as a punishment, there was plenty to do in the yard, we had swings and a slide. I wasn't trying to make him suffer. I was only wanting to control the environment to meet my need for safety.

Now many parents say, "Well, isn't the child likely to see that as a punishment ? " Well, if it has been intended as a punishment in the past, if the child has had a lot of experience seeing people as punitive, yes, they could still see it as a punishment. The main thing, though, is that we, the parents, are conscious of this difference, and that if we use force, we're certain that it is to protect and not to punish.

One way of remembering the purpose of the protective use of force is to see the difference between controlling the child and controlling the environment. In punishment we're trying to control the child by making the child feel bad about what they've done, to create an internal shame, guilt, or fear for what they have done.

In the protective use of force, our intent is not to control the child ; it's to control the environment. To protect our needs until such time as we can have the quality of communication with the other person that's really necessary. It's somewhat like putting screens on our house to protect us from being bitten by mosquitoes. It's a protective use of force. We control the environment to prevent things happening that we don't want to happen.

Supportive Communities

Now, the way of parenting that I'm advocating here is quite different from how most people are parenting. And it's going to be difficult to consider radically different options in a world where punishment is so prevalent, and where you are likely to be misinterpreted if you don't use punishment and other coercive forms of parental behavior. It really helps people immensely if they are part of a supportive community that understands the concept of parenting I'm talking about, where they have the support to continue to do this in a world that doesn't often support it.

I know that I was always much better able to stay with what I'm now talking about if I was getting a lot of empathy myself from a supportive community, empathy for how hard it can be to be a parent at times. How easy it is to fall into old patterns. When I had other parents similarly trying to connect with their children as I was, it was very supportive to be able to talk to them, and to hear their frustrations, to have them hear mine. And I noticed that the more that I was part of such a community, the better able I was to stay with this process with my children, even under difficult conditions.

And one of the rewarding things that happened that was very encouraging and enriching, was a message I received from my daughter when she was very small. It was on a Sunday morning, the only time of the week when I could relax, a very precious time for me.

Now, on this particular Sunday morning, a couple called me up and asked if I would be willing to see them in counseling. They had a crisis in their relationship, and wanted me to work with them. And I agreed to do this without really looking inside myself and seeing what my own needs were, and how I was resenting their intrusion on my time to relax. While I had them in the living room counseling them, the doorbell rang and the police were bringing in a young woman for me to see. I had also been seeing her in counseling, and they had found her down on the railroad tracks. That was her way of letting me know she wanted to see me. She was too shy to call up and ask for another appointment. This was her way, sitting on the railroad tracks, of letting me know she was in distress. She knew the train schedule better than anyone in town, so she knew the police would pick her up before the train got her.

So then the police left, and I had this young woman in the kitchen crying, and the couple in the living room, and I was going back and forth trying to lovingly counsel both. And while I was doing this, walking from one room to the other, looking at my watch, hoping I would still have time afterward to have some time to myself, the three children upstairs started fighting. So I bounded up the stairs, and I found something fascinating. I might write this up in a scientific paper some day: the effect of altitude on maniac behavior. Because you see, downstairs I was a very loving person, giving love to this couple, giving love to the young woman in the other room, but one flight of stairs up and I was a maniac.

I said to my children: "What's the matter with you? Can't you see that I have hurting people downstairs? Now get in your rooms!" And each went in their rooms and slammed the door just loud enough that I couldn't prove it was a slam, and when it happened the first time I got more outraged, and the second time even more. But fortunately the third time it happened, I don't know why, but it helped me see the humor in the situation. How easy it was for me to be loving of these people downstairs, but how quickly I could get brutal with my own family upstairs.

I took a deep breath and I went first in my oldest son's room and told him I was sad that I was taking out some feelings on him that I was afraid I really had in relation to the people downstairs. He understood, he just said : "It's OK, Dad. Nothing big." I went in my youngest son's room and got a pretty similar response from him. And when I went in my daughter's room and told her that I felt sad at the way I had talked to her, she came over and put her head on my shoulder and said : "It's OK, Daddy. Nobody's perfect."

What a precious message to hear. Yes, my children appreciate my efforts to relate to them in a caring way, in a compassionate way, an empathic way. But how relieving it is that they can understand my humanness and how difficult it can sometimes be.

So in closing I offer you that reassuring advice given to me by my daughter, that nobody's perfect, to remember that anything that's worth doing is worth doing poorly. And the job of parenting, of course, is extremely worth doing, but we're going to do it poorly at times. If we're going to be brutal with ourselves when we're not perfect parents, our children are going to suffer for that.

I often tell the parents that I'm working with that hell is having children and thinking there's such a thing as a good parent. That if every time we're less than perfect, we're going to blame ourselves and attack ourselves, our children are not going to benefit from that. So the goal I would suggest is not to be perfect parents, it's to become progressively less stupid parents — by learning from each time that we're not able to give our children the quality of understanding that they need, that we're not able to express ourselves honestly. In my experience, each of these times usually means that we're not getting the emotional support we need as parents, in order to give our children what they need.

We can only really give in a loving way to the degree

that we are receiving similar love and understanding. So that's why I strongly recommend that we look at how we might create a supportive community for ourselves among our friends and others, who can give us the understanding we need to be present to our children in a way that will be good for them and good for us.

I hope that something I've said here has helped you grow closer to becoming the parent you would like to be.

The Four-Part Nonviolent Communication Process

Clearly expressing
how **I am**
without blaming
or criticizing

Empathically receiving
how **you are**
without hearing
blame or criticism

OBSERVATIONS

1. What I observe (*see, hear, remember, imagine, free from my evaluations*) that does or does not contribute to my well-being:
"*When I (see, hear) …*"

1. What you observe (*see, hear, remember, imagine, free from your evaluations*) that does or does not contribute to your well-being:
"*When you see/hear…*"

(*Sometimes unspoken when offering empathy*)

FEELINGS

2. How I feel (*emotion or sensation rather than thought*) in relation to what I observe:
"*I feel…*"

2. How you feel (*emotion or sensation rather than thought*) in relation to what you observe:
"*You feel…*"

NEEDS

3. What I need or value *(rather than a preference, or a specific action)* that causes my feelings:
   "…because I need/value…"

3. What you need or value *(rather than a preference, or a specific action)* that causes your feelings:
   "…because you need/value …"

Clearly requesting that which would enrich **my** life without demanding

Empathically receiving that which would enrich **your** life without hearing any demand

REQUESTS

4. The concrete actions I would like taken:
   "Would you be willing to…?"

4. The concrete actions you would like taken:
   "Would you like…?"
   (Sometimes unspoken when offering empathy)

© Marshall B. Rosenberg. For more information about Marshall B. Rosenberg or the Center for Nonviolent Communication, please visit www.CNVC.org.

Some Basic Feelings We All Have

Feelings when needs are fulfilled

- Amazed
- Fulfilled
- Joyous
- Stimulated
- Comfortable
- Glad
- Moved
- Surprised
- Confident
- Hopeful
- Optimistic
- Thankful
- Eager
- Inspired
- Proud
- Touched
- Energetic
- Intrigued
- Relieved
- Trustful

Feelings when needs are not fulfilled

- Angry
- Discouraged
- Hopeless
- Overwhelmed
- Annoyed
- Distressed
- Impatient
- Puzzled
- Concerned
- Embarrassed
- Irritated
- Reluctant
- Confused
- Frustrated
- Lonely
- Sad
- Disappointed
- Helpless
- Nervous
- Uncomfortable

Some Basic Needs We All Have

Autonomy

- Choosing dreams/goals/values
- Choosing plans for fulfilling one's dreams, goals, values

Celebration

- Celebrating the creation of life and dreams fulfilled
- Celebrating losses: loved ones, dreams, etc. (mourning)

Integrity

- Authenticity
- Creativity
- Meaning
- Self-worth

Physical Nurturance

- Air
- Food
- Movement, exercise
- Protection from life-threatening forms of life: viruses,

bacteria, insects, predatory animals

- Rest
- Sexual Expression
- Shelter
- Touch
- Water

Play

- Fun
- Laughter

Spiritual Communion

- Beauty
- Harmony
- Inspiration
- Order
- Peace

Interdependence

- Acceptance
- Appreciation
- Closeness
- Community
- Consideration
- Contribution to the enrichment of life
- Emotional Safety
- Empathy
- Honesty (the empowering honesty that enables us to learn

from our limitations）

- Love
- Reassurance
- Respect
- Support
- Trust
- Understanding

《非暴力沟通》（修订版）

当我们褪去隐蔽的精神暴力，
爱将自然流露。
非暴力沟通入门主书，
必读经典，畅销多年。

一种生命的语言

《非暴力沟通·"无错区"教室》

21节课，18个课程单元带领师生共用体验式、可视化的方式创建和谐的教室氛围，自主学习和自行化解冲突的能力。

首次将非暴力沟通
应用到教室内的详细课程计划书

《非暴力沟通亲子篇》

非暴力沟通在亲子教养方面的引导指南，《正面管教》《高效能人士的七个习惯》《非暴力沟通》三大作者隆重推荐。

用非暴力沟通的"七把钥匙"创建家长和孩子之间的尊重和合作，开启化解家庭冲突，促进合作的沟通模式

《教室里的非暴力沟通》

非暴力沟通中心认证的国际培训师教你如何在学校中灵活运用非暴力沟通。

用沟通技巧 + 观点引导 + 具体方法
教你如何释放孩子天性中的学习渴望